Rich,

Thanks for all
your hard work
and good luck on
the journey.

Cheers,

# A FOOL
# WITH A TOOL

*A Battle-Hardened Guide to Sales Transformation*

## BLAIR GOULET

*Co-Founder of INK Sales Strategy Software*

Lulu Publishing Services rev. date: 06/17/2016

# CONTENTS

# INTRODUCTION

## "A FOOL WITH A TOOL IS STILL A FOOL."
### -Grady Booch (Software Developer)

If we all look in the mirror, there is a pretty good chance that we have all invested in some form of tool or technology in our lives to solve a problem. There is also a very good chance that it did not change the outcome. Examples include acquiring CRM to help sales results or an app for your iPhone to help you lose weight or most Infomercial products. Business leaders, when faced with a daunting problem and the need for transformation, have been known to invest in tools or quick fixes rather than do root causal work to understand the real issue or to invest in process improvement and transformative change. Why?

Well, we do like our toys. 75% of businesses in North America have acquired some kind of CRM tool. Over 50% would state that they acquired the tool to improve how they sell. A very high percentage are not using the tool properly or for its intended purpose, and a Gartner study indicated over 50% do not use the tool at all! Despite what Marc Benioff (the outspoken CEO of Salesforce.com) says, CRM or sales force automation tools will seldom be responsible for you winning a deal. A database tool like CRM allows you to look in the rear view mirror after you have recorded what happened; but it will add limited value without the structure that you need to bring to the party. If you have defined processes, software tools will support and enable, but you need to start with process.

The reality is tools are easy answers and it is more fun to buy tangible assets. Root cause and strategy work is hard and requires certain skills. There is also the perception that it takes more time and money. We are all looking for more immediate gratification in both our business and personal lives and thus investing in quick fixes is logical. Unfortunately, they seldom yield the desired results.

We are in the business of developing and delivering software, consulting and professional services. We create software tools that add value as stand alone solutions, but there is a value multiplier when coupled with effective process and the other required elements. Regardless of how good the underlying software may be and how it may be the best thing since cold beer at resolving the root business problem, there needs to be a linkage to existing (or new) process to extract the potential value.

**A Fool with a Tool** focuses on the realities of the current selling environment and pressure points on sales leaders and reps. As many organizations seek to transform results, many areas of the sales business need to transform first. We are going to tell this story with a focus on Sales Strategy. Sales Strategy can be defined in both the Macro and Micro sense. Macro being the Sales Strategy of a company and micro being the Sales Strategy for an individual deal or pursuit. Strategy is critical to transformation and tools support the execution plan.

Tools are good things. They can support productivity gains, improve workflow, consistency, skill development and the ability to get access to timely/accurate information to list a few benefits. We believe in tools as a critical component to transformation. That said, we have all been fools at some point in our lives.

Have fun.

"If you want to teach people a new way of thinking, don't bother trying to teach them. Instead, give them a tool, the use of which will teach them a new way of thinking."

-Richard Buckminster Fuller

# PART A

# REALITY

# ONE
# SELLING IN THE 3.0 WORLD

Selling has always been hard work and it is getting harder. 2008 onward have brought on significant macro economic headwinds that have materially impacted the markets in which most of us compete. The strong will survive and those with weak balance sheets or poor business models will be acquired or go by the wayside. The trends that are evolving in the world of complex sales and the dynamics going on inside many organizations are continuing to put more pressure on sales organizations in a hyper competitive world.

I am not trying to be negative, but the dynamics of our markets are forcing both change and the requirement to do things faster and better. Organizations that have strong balance sheets (or leveraged) are buying growth through acquisitions. For most that luxury may not exist and thus organic growth is a requirement. Organic growth may also be a dream without the strategic plan that creates the strategic flow between Corporate Strategy, Marketing Strategy and the corresponding Sales Strategy.

Is there the required focus and alignment to enable the Sales organization to maximize effectiveness and enable the broader Corporate Strategy? Data would suggest not. This creates a real opportunity to leverage sales effectiveness as a vehicle for differentiation and growth.

# What We Have Heard

In over 200 interviews with Executives and Sales Leaders in the past few years, we have noticed common areas of concern and priority that came up again and again.

**Sales Challenges:**

- **Need for Organic Growth** is constant and a heavy burden on Sales organizations.
- **Declining Win Rates** and increasing numbers of "No Decisions" impacts Revenue and Cost of Sale.
- **Increased Cost of Sale** because of longer sales cycles plus chasing poorly qualified or the wrong deals.
- **Growing Complexity** on the "Sell" side and the "Buy" side is forcing a higher level of skills and preparation.
- **Predictability Issues** based on clear understanding of where we are positioned and knowledge (or lack there of) of the client's decision process creates internal challenges and credibility issues for Sales.
- The **ability to differentiate** our offering has become more difficult in a hyper-competitive market that has significant price pressures.

We ask CEO's and Executives to rate the effectiveness of their sales organization on scale of 1-10 [10 being high]. We have never had an answer higher than a 6. The answer to the second level question varies, but themes are usually around lack of results, skill gaps, transparency and predictability of results.

# Market Trends

Trends have emerged in the past 4-5 years that absolutely are impacting (or should) how we need to sell our products and services.

**Are these trends impacting you?**

- **Increased Governance** from prospective clients. Their processes are more detailed (RFI, RFP), are more scrutinized internally or have high approval hurdles (ROI, IRR).
- **Risk Aversion**. Decision teams or decision-makers are unlikely to make risky, career threatening moves if the status quo is good enough.
- **Consensus Decisions**. Formal decision-makers increasingly look to teams of individuals from different functions and levels for input to reduce personal risk and drive personal attachment to decisions.
- **Buying Process**. Clients have access to vast amounts of information and both educate themselves plus define needs before they engage vendors. Vendors are showing up half way through the movie when the discussion is now about price.
- **Vendor Knowledge**. Clients expect vendors to be knowledgeable about their industry and about their company because they do not have the time to educate vendors. The expectations of you are rising daily.
- **No Decisions**. Data would suggest that if you have 100 deals in your funnel today, more than half of them would become "No Decisions". This relates to risk aversion, complexity and challenges of groups to reach consensus.

# Sales Factoids

Various groups and ongoing studies track global data on Sales organizations that become a good form of comparison.

- **48%** of Sales Reps (and declining) **achieve their annual quota.**
- 85% of Companies **raise their quotas** on an annual basis.
- 50% of Companies would state that they could define how they sell.
- **46% of "Forecasted" deals close** with 54% as losses or no decisions
- Only **10% of deals close as Forecasted** (Right date and size).
- Sales Training expenditures have declined 5 years in a row.
- 87% of Sales Training concepts are not used within 30 days.
- 75% of North American companies have invested in CRM and less than 50% of them use the tool properly or at all.

**Sales Effectiveness is declining!** Investments in people and process are declining. Investments in tools are increasing with limited returns.

# Changing Buying Process

As Sales Leaders or Sales Reps, we tend to think about our Sales Process, but think little about the clients Buying Process. The point is that based on all the things that are going on in our clients world, they have actually changed how they buy products and services. These changes are subtle but impactful on us as sellers.

**CEB** has done extensive research on this topic and I will highlight a few key data points that are impactful to us and how we sell.

Access to information allows clients to self-educate like never before if they are looking to make change. Vendors are the most dominant source of information.

If a client is going to make change, they need to determine what they require based on the problem they are trying to resolve. This will begin as a feature / function exercise.

**SAMPLE BUYING PROCESS**

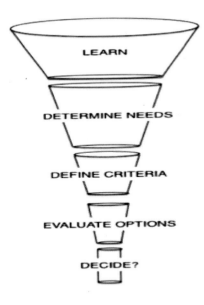

As clients now invite vendors to the party, they need to define the criteria by which you will judge those that come. This is likely where the RFP is issued.

Now the options get evaluated and a short list occurs. Criteria may get more detailed, prioritized and measurable.

Time to make a decision or does the status quo prevail?

It is no secret that clients don't really want to talk to sales people. **The average sales rep does not get invited in until the Buying Process is 57% complete.**

# Complexity and Commoditization

I have a theory that I have been floating out there that increasing Complexity in your clients' environments actually leads to Commoditization of vendors' goods and services. Let me explain and you can decide for yourself.

It is easy to get agreement that your clients' world is getting more complex and as things roll down hill, your world gets more complex. I believe there is direct connection between growing complexity, the need to make decisions and commoditization.

Think about your clients' world. They are all being asked to do more with less, create better business outcomes, faster and with reduced resources [people, $, etc.]. Making decisions is more challenging because of the complexity of options and number of stakeholders who are involved in the process. The stakes are also higher based on both personal and corporate risk. But with all that in the blender, you need to make a decision. So, what might your client do?

When faced with these challenges, clients try and simplify so they can actually make a decision. They may try and net out very different and complex options from vendors to the lowest common denominators. If they can make decision options look similar and comparable, then they may actually be able to make a decision. The side benefit may be commoditization of vendors. If we can make them all fit in the same box from a criteria perspective, then we can focus the discussion and decision on price. Our clients tell us they feel this all the time and this may be a reason why.

# The Theory of Good Enough

Building on the previous hypothesis, let me now share "The Theory of Good Enough". When faced with the need to make a decision and having a myriad of complex choices, we may select the solution that is Good Enough. We do this in our personal lives every day. Whether you are buying a car, fridge, phone or toothbrush, we make rational and emotional trade-offs daily. In all likelihood, there is always a more expensive, feature rich, higher quality option that we could select. If it is not critical to our life, chances are we may settle for good enough and get moving. Using a phone as an example; emotion or psychological decision making factors come into play and we do not settle. See iPhone sales for details.

Does this really happen in a business-to-business world? I have been involved in complex, multi-year sales cycles of mission critical technology. Even in that world, we saw clients settling all the time. That said, we would always try to influence [or guide] decision-making criteria, so they did not settle for good enough because the consequences could be catastrophic.

Depending on your strategy and/or value proposition, this theory could be a risk for you or actually used for your advantage. Let me illustrate the latter point. As a vendor, you may be the "good enough" vendor and thus you want to steer the decision in that direction. I saw this recently with a large technology company. They were beating competitors in their non-core space by offering a complimentary solution that was not best in class, but it was good enough. They were trying to educate clients that they had already made the strategic decision [with them] and that in the adjacent space they should just buy good enough. It is working.

Either way you choose to approach this challenge, the core thing you need to do is either educate or re-educate your clients about what they need and the criteria by which to judge the vendors that compete for their business.

# Risk Aversion

Risk aversion contains many impactful components that hurt sales organizations in the 3.0 Selling World. Stakes are higher for everybody and the decision governance hurdles are higher than ever before.

There are a number of factors at play here. When we are being asked to do more with less, we are more comfortable with the status quo. Unless the pain is overwhelming to the point we can no longer live with it or the gain opportunity is so immense, we will stay where we are. Clients become convinced that the status quo is the safest, least expensive place to be. In general, that is an incorrect assumption, but leads to inactivity or no decisions. One data point to keep in mind; we are 3x as likely to act because of the Pain problem versus to seize the Gain. They are not created equal.

Risk aversion has changed clients' processes. Whether it is the number of RFP's / RFI's or the rise of 3rd Party Consultants to help with said RFP's; these activities take longer and are more complex. The other major shift is the number of people involved in the clients' decision-making process. CEB research into this area would suggest there are between 5-6 people involved in the decision process in a complex transaction. I have seen 20+ in consensus based committee decisions. We were all schooled to find the decision-maker in the deal. The reality is that one person is becoming a unicorn. To be certain, all the people involved do not have equal voices, but they do have voices.

What is also certain is those people will show up from different functions, roles and hierarchy with very different perspectives, mandates and biases. The challenge this creates is the ability for people to actually reach consensus and make a decision. If there are more than 6 people involved, there is only a 31% chance they will move forward and make a decision.

If there are a couple of things that they *can* agree upon, it is either to do nothing or to choose the lower cost / good enough solution. Once again, these could either work to your advantage or disadvantage depending on your strategy or positioning. It should give you something to ponder as you look at some of your pursuits in the way of strategic options.

# What Are You Really Selling

This may sound like a trick or very simple question. The answer resides in this concept of the status quo. When we show up as sales people, in general, our clients are firmly entrenched in the status quo. So, what is it we are really selling?

We are selling CHANGE. We are trying to get our clients thinking differently about their current situation or problem. Until they do that, we are just talking. This is very specific skill and it will create very different sounding commercial conversations with your clients. It also changes your strategic focus because we know they are not inclined to make change.

If we are really selling change, then who is our primary COMPETITOR? We all have strong and worthy competitors in the markets in which we compete. The answer here is our clients themselves because of their risk aversion and the preference towards the status quo or potentially to do it themselves. This DIY mindset could be about self-preservation, but when you think about that internal business case, it is in conflict with "doing more with less".

This will vary by market and client, but we have seen this dynamic play out the same way regardless of the industry or country that we are in.

# Getting From A to B

The journey from A to B is a reference for moving from the Current Reality to transforming to the Desired State. My objective here is to give you some things to think about that cause you to percolate more on your Current State. I would encourage you to take a step backward first.

In a **Marketing Executive Board** study, less than 30% of companies (with their hand over their heart) would admit to have a true Value Proposition. Investments that would support and enable sales may start with your proven Value Based Positioning. There are some "Quick Wins" you may be able to find. "Quick Fixes" are desired, but unlikely. Real work is going to be required.

Assuming that organic growth is a top priority, then take a deep breath and build a Sales Strategy that is focused, aligned and has the proper investment. You need to understand the current state and any root issues before you can create and design the desired state. Think about what the facts tell you about your:

- **Value Proposition**
- **Sales Process**
- **Structure, Resources, Productivity**
- **Governance Processes and Controls**
- **Technology and Tools**

There is a specific sequence as to why we have suggested them in this order that we will discuss in the next Chapter. This will help create understanding and also guide your priorities. You will notice that Tools are last on the list.

# Summary Notes

Growth is
required and Sales
Effectiveness is
Declining

Complexity is
increasing for the
Buyer and Seller

Client Risk Aversion
is a very impactful
to our results and
how we sell

# Exercise

Grab a piece of paper (or your team and a white board). Answer the following questions:

1. You talk to your customers and your peers daily about what is going in the world of Sales or revenue generation. What are common themes you are seeing that are different than the common ones we referenced?
2. What trends are evolving in your Industry that may impact how you sell?
3. What are Key Performance Indicator's (KPI's) or measures of sales effectiveness for your business and what do the trends tell you?

# TWO

# HOW DO YOU SELL

Sounds like a simple question – right? Only 50% of businesses would state that they even have a Sales Process or could define how they sell. Within that 50% who say they could, you will find the cast from the "The Good, The Bad and The Ugly".

In the past few years, through hundreds of interviews with Executives, Sales Leaders and Sales Reps, it is clear that the majority of organizations could not answer this question. "How You Sell" is the Sales Process that defines the what, how, and who for your sales teams.

Like many things in life, we do things in a certain way because we have always done things that way. That may imply that it is not broken, but it is also does not imply that it is maximizing potential or effectiveness. The world is moving far too fast for things to stay constant for too long.

To be clear, the belief that we are putting forward is that the ability to identify "how you sell" or "could/should sell" is a journey of innovation and differentiation. With that level of understanding, then the discussion about structure, training, governance and tools becomes much clearer.

# Why You Should Care

As a starting point, "How You Sell" is the center point of Sales differentiation and decision-making. We believe that a Sales Process is the basis of competitive advantage and the foundation for other Sales Strategy decisions. Don't believe us? Research firms have uncovered some interesting facts and trends that emphasize and build upon the point.

The Chally Group did comprehensive research on "why people BUY from you to begin with" and the results were interesting. 100,000 B2B Buyers rated "How You Sell" as the most important factor in vendor selection over price, quality or service.

The seminal research behind CEB's book "The Challenger Sale", approached the topic in a different way, but found very similar results. CEB was focused on the key drivers of Client Loyalty. "The Sales Experience" has the #1 impact on customer loyalty over value to price ratio, product / service and your brand combined.

There are a couple of things worth noting here. First, the other factors such as a quality company, having great products and services plus being price competitive are critically important. These are table stakes to even be in the game. If you are in the game, then what you should remember is that you can compete and differentiate based on "how you sell". The second thing to remember that is consistent in every study ever done on this topic is that *price* is always the lowest rated factor of why they buy from you or stay loyal to you. If they bought from you because of price, they will leave for the same reason.

# Segmentation, Targeting & Positioning

This is your traditional marketing STP. "How You Sell" will be materially impacted by whom you sell to. Duh right? A key reason for a growing Cost of Sale and Sales Cycle Length is selling to the wrong prospects. Based on how you create value, there is Segmentation, Targeting & Positioning work to be done up front to define the Characteristics of an ideal customer.

High-level Segmentation may include size, geography and industry vertical. As you go deeper, areas like the incumbent competitor, contract expiry and other more specific characteristics come into view. In a past life we were selling enterprise software and one of our criteria was the age of the CEO and if their retirement was on the horizon. We knew from experience that the CEO was very unlikely to take on massive risks that close to his/her career finish line. Think about risk aversion and the status quo again.

Targeting opens up fresh discussions about the Roles within the prospective organization that are impacted by your products and services. Working with a client recently the discussion shifted away from the usual suspects to Influencers from other functions. Their traditional targeting was CEO, CIO and COO. What we determined was that Marketing, given the consumer facing technology our client offered, could be a key mobilizer of change. That said, your Positioning to each of these Target groups is different. Fundamentally, based on their mandates and what they care about, they speak very different languages.

Positioning is also known as Value-Based Positioning or your Value Proposition. A lengthier topic than we go into here, but the simple concept of Positioning is about your unique and measurable value. I have seen this represented by an equation:

$$Value = Quality/Price$$

As consumers, we make these simple decisions every day. Based on the Quality you see in a good or service, you will either pay more or less. The higher the perceived quality then the greater the price elasticity.

Your Value Proposition can or should be a key driver of "How You Sell" your goods and services.

This is relatively basic advice, but you may want to do some work to refresh your thinking on this topic. One of our clients did what I thought was some benchmark work in this area. They did the following, which may be of value to you:

1. *Build characteristics of an Ideal Customer based on your Segmentation and your "sweet spot"*
2. *Rank and Prioritize those characteristics*
3. *Filter your Territories based on new Priorities to determine your calling Priorities and Marketing focus*
4. *Determine your Targets within the Accounts on how your unique Value supports and enables each stakeholder*
5. *Create Positioning Statements for each Target stakeholder*

# How Are You Being Judged

Clients will have relatively common criteria by which they are going to judge the vendors that show up to the party. They may formally define the decision-making criteria or it may be more casual based on the complexity and cost of your goods and services.

In the Value Proposition Refinement work we do with clients, one of things I always do is talk to 6+ customers. I have standardized questions, but one of the key things I want to understand is "why" they bought from which vendor, the criteria they used to judge vendors and the process they followed. The outputs are impactful to value creation, but also to How You Sell. I have found several common themes over the years:

- Clients always think about the best Feature / Function fit based on their needs first, which is quickly followed by a Price to Value reference
- With second and third level questions, you usually find the final decision was about risk levels, customer service, cultural fit, strategic fit or other criteria that they determined to be **most** important when they went through the buying / sales process
- Price is seldom / never the primary selection criteria and even if they thought it was, it is unlikely the reason they would now stay loyal

How You Are You Being Judged is a critical area to understand that can have profound impact on Positioning and Sales. Let me offer a little free consulting and some tools to how may approach this opportunity.

I would encourage you start by modeling and gaining agreement on the common criteria by which you are being judged. You may also call this the Decision-Making Criteria or the Factors of Competition in an industry.

If you are familiar with the concept of *Blue Ocean Strategy,* I would encourage you to borrow a tool called a Strategy Canvas. A Strategy Canvas allows you to visualize your Strategy based on your Value, measured against your primary competitors. On the X-Axis are the Factors of Competition in your industry or how you are consistently judged. On the Y-Axis, you will create a Low to High Scale. You will then subjectively and / or objectively plot your positioning on each of these Factors against your primary competitors. For the first time, you may be able to visually see your Positioning, for better or worse.

You are being judged by these factors every day. Can you prove your current positioning? Can you measure it? This may be easier than you think, but will require you to think differently about how you measure and prove. If you understand where you really are, then you create an opportunity to potentially Innovate or change your Positioning to create valuable differentiation.

I have seen this work several times and the results can be magical. It can cause an organization to look differently at itself [which creates a renewed confidence], position itself much differently [internally and externally] and ultimately may have a profound impact on sales results.

# What Are Your Key Sales Activities

This question sounds pretty tactical. It can be, but understanding what you do and what really leads to success, can impact Sales Strategy.

"What" defines the core activities that should be consistent within most sales cycles. The sequence may be different depending on the opportunity, but what they are should be pretty similar across different products, teams and sales reps.

The exercise to understand "What" will lead to many "why" questions as to how this became the standard. In doing work with many companies on this topic, the "what" is often generic and inconsistent with the real inconsistency occurring at the Rep and Team level based on the style and experience of your people.

Determining what you do is an exercise in differentiation, value creation and innovation based on an underlying belief that you can be different in how you sell.

Create detail on purpose. If there are things to be done that require focus, process and skills to be good at (let alone differentiate), then understand those "what's". The objective is not to create complexity or a 15 Step Sales Process, but to truly understand all the activities that occur from Prospecting through to deal Closure. These activities all provide data on effectiveness and clues as to how you may be able to Innovate and Differentiate.

Start by answering these questions:

1. **What are the activities** that are reflective of a typical Sales Cycle from Initiation through to Closure?
2. Would your Managers and Reps be aligned on **what the key activities are**?
3. **What do you do that makes you different** or adds unique value in your Sales Process?

4.  What do you do that gives you the greatest chance of success?
5.  Does your internal data support your theory?

You now have a picture of what you do in the way of key activities. Some of these are your decision and some of these are industry-standards and thus imposed upon you. Let me give you a couple of examples.

Technology sales reps often default to doing a demo of their shiny widget as early in the sales process as they can. It is viewed as a sign of interest and thus if you do a demo early, then you can build momentum. This is followed quickly by a price quotation or proposal. These process steps are your decision and come with lots of self-imposed challenges.

In an industry that I was in, there were process steps that were imposed upon us as standards. RFP's, 2-day full solution suite demos, client site visits to name three. Whether we wanted to do these steps or not, they were imposed upon us and we had no choice but to comply or be removed. They became discrete steps in our Sales Process because there were defined skills, process, and tools required to consistently be good at these activities, let alone differentiated.

# How Do You Do Them

Building on my last point, you can further Define or Refine How You Sell based on "How" you conduct your key sales activities.

If you can clearly define the sequence of activities that make up "What" you do (with some understanding of "why"), then the real work begins with understanding or creating the "How". This implies it is understood, documented and that resources are deployed against this component of Sales Strategy. Resources include your sales structure, hiring the right people to execute the "how", training on the "how", processes and controls that measure and reinforce the "how" and the tools that enable the "how".

If you have drawn what your activities are in a linear fashion, then make a list below each item of "How" exactly you do that. To illustrate, in virtually every B2B sale, one of the sales activities is the creation of some form of proposal, which could be an RFP response in the extreme case. The question is how do your proposals maximize value, differentiate and increase your chances of success?

Innovation and Differentiation can occur as you look at the last three questions. You can change the game and create a different sales experience based on how you approach your Sales Process. You can change the sequence of events to change your chance of success. If you have a bulletproof reference list of clients, don't save that card until the end. Play it early as part of your Process or Strategy to both create value for your prospect and momentum for your deal. It is a good test for the prospect to see if they are where you think they are and your reference may actually get them thinking differently about what they need, their criteria and the vendors they should consider. We have seen RFP's stop and the process change to a sole source discussion based on changing how you sell.

# Who Is Involved

Complex Sales is a team sport. Sales Reps sometimes feel like they are alone. I have heard Managers say they wish that their Reps had the confidence to take more control and ownership of the opportunity. Clarity of the "What" and "How" will create confidence. To be clear, Reps should own opportunities and everyone else (including the CEO) is a resource to be used at the right point in time.

As you are creating the "How", there is an element of "Who" as it relates to ownership and support of the various activities. Clearly defined expectations, training, process and tools will help enable the team to clearly understand their role. This also helps minimize fire drills, "not my job" perspectives and helps set priorities for people.

If you have the right resources, which have been properly trained and they have the appropriate tools to do their job, then they should be comfortable wearing the captains "C". This may be nirvana for you or there may be cultural barriers that prevent this from happening. It may be a higher bar that you strive to achieve because it makes the Sales Leaders job easier and is critical for growth

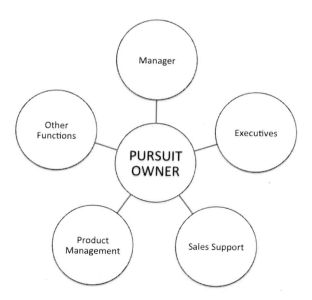

# Your Vision

If I asked you [or one of your reps] what your vision for a specific client is, how would you or they answer the question? The typical response I hear from a Rep is that we would like to sell $xx worth of XYZ product by this specific date. Sales Leaders typically talk about vendor of choice or trusted advisor status, which are less tactical. I am driving at something different here, which forces us to think differently about our approach.

Your clients are concerned about what is important to them and how they get measured. This sounds more like revenue growth, cost reduction, improved profitability, risk reduction or decreased time to market. What if your vision for your client was to help reduce their time to market by 10%? Assuming you had an idea or vision of how to do that and you knew it was a priority for them, how would this change your sales approach? Do you think you would get a different audience or reception?

If you are curious as to how this may change your pursuits, I would offer you this data point. If you are the one who creates the vision for the client, your chances of being successful are 75%. Clients will reward innovation. This will create different sounding conversations with your sales teammates. What is your vision for the client? You begin to think different, approach opportunities differently and selling differently.

# The Business Case For Change

If we show up at the beginning versus half way through the Buying Process, then what we are selling is Change. An opportunity for us is to partner with our Client to work together to build the business case for change. There are implications to this statement beginning with trust, credibility and the client understanding the potential impact of investing in change.

By my definition, the Business Case for Change is different than an ROI. An ROI implies there is a solution on the table and you are comparing the cost of the problem with the benefit of the solution. I believe the Business Case for Change can be a differentiated early stage sales activity that creates high value for your client and differentiation for you. If you are truly working with them and you know what you are looking for and what to ask for, then at a certain point you will know more about the clients' situation than they do. You are armed and dangerous. The Case for Change is the quantification of the impact of the current problem or opportunity.

In some sales circles this may also be called a "Diagnostic Process". This is a qualified investment by your sales teams in the right opportunities. If done well and appropriately, not only do you differentiate but it has been proven to dramatically improve Win Rates.

One of the questions I ask sales organizations on this topic, relates to their understanding of the business problem they believe they solve for clients. "If you had unrestricted access to a clients' organization, people and data, where would you go, who would you talk to, what would be looking for to prove the business problem exists and worth solving?" I often hear, "that is great question." You can visualize the thoughtful look on their face as they think about the answer.

How would you answer the question?

If you work with them on the Business Case, which will evolve into an ROI once your solution shows up, then it does a few powerful things for you. The first helps address the status quo issue. It has been proven that if there is a compelling reason for making change, and then it materially increases the chances [by 30%] that they will make a decision. Secondarily, it also improves your positioning and chances of being successful. You may actually know more about what is going on within the clients' organization than they do. You are now armed and dangerous.

# Tactical Playbook

I define the Tactical Playbook as a prescriptive set of moves or requests that your sales force will make at various points of the sales cycle. The defining characteristics are that they add Value to the client and create Momentum for the opportunity.

Think about this way. When you show up, the client may be imbedded in the status quo. Your opportunity is going nowhere unless at least one person in the client organization is prepared to use some political capital to try and mobilize change. What are the Tactics that you can use that add value for them to help them in this process?

Examples could include asking them to partner in the Business Case for Change, participate in a qualified Proof of Concept, to call some references with peers who had the same problem or to give you data that will allow you to build an ROI.

Less powerful examples I hear all the time are to attend a product demo or to agree to another meeting. Other meetings can pass our Value and Momentum test if they spend some political capital to invite other stakeholders to the meeting. In all of these examples, the client has to physically do something, which also makes these tactics a good test to see if they have bought in or not.

As the opportunity advances, what we know is more people will be showing up on the client side, which immediately makes this more complex and slows things down. It also changes the tactics in the playbook. The ROI model is now complete and verified with the client, they may get on a plane to do a client site visit or corporate visit, you work with them to build the roadmap to reach consensus or you give them an initial project / implementation plan to review. Again, these are all things the client physically has to do or participate in.

You are looking to increase your chances of success with each move you make. Your sales reps will not just intuitively do all of these things and they are not all created equal as it pertains to Value and Momentum creation. I would encourage you to overlay your tactics against your new process to determine what you can /should be doing at each phase. I would then document each Tactic and lay out the process flow and then train your sales teams on your Tactical Playbook.

# Innovation and Differentiation

The output of a well-considered Sales Strategy and corresponding Sales Process is the opportunity to Innovate and Differentiate in How You Sell. Your critical differentiator could be the sales experience itself. If you can innovate, then you can differentiate.

There is a tool we use to help clients innovate and differentiate their Sales Process. The **Force Field** is a powerful exercise that we have created for clients. It opens the aperture much wider to understand how they could or should sell for both differentiation and increased success. How do these factors impact how you can innovate or differentiate?

Overlaid against the "What" and the "How", the **Force Field** is a series of exercises and questions to gain a better understanding of:

1.  Your Value Proposition and how you can imbed your unique value in how you sell.
2.  How Clients Want to Buy goods and services like yours and how you make it easy or difficult for them to buy from you?
3.  What are the Decision Making Standards in your industry and (if this is how you are going to be judged) does how you sell align and enable success?
4.  What Industry or Competitive influences impact how you sell and how do you work with or around those to your advantage?

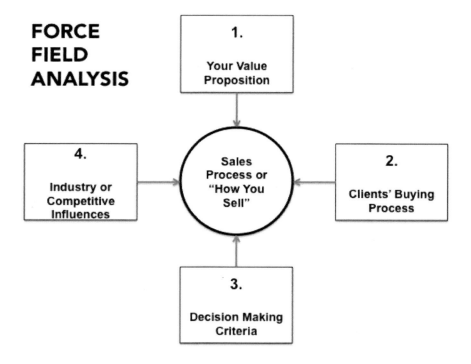

The visual above shows how to work through the exercise to help you think differently about your sales experience.

We have seen this in action and we have created some examples.

The ability to innovate and differentiate comes from situational understanding. We encounter many situations where companies, teams or reps attempt to differentiate, but in reality they are really guessing.

How would your success chances change if you were not guessing?

**Leverage Your Value Proposition.** One of our clients is a large software company. A key value creator and differentiator for them is world-class customer service. 98% customer satisfaction leads to 99% customer retention. It is the center of their business model. One of the tactical sales process investments they made was to move references or referrals up in the sales process by providing an entire customer list. It is a great test for prospects to get them investing time early in a sales cycle. More importantly, they can either dramatically improve their positioning or have competitors removed based on the voice of their customers.

**How Clients Buy.** The first assumption we often make is that clients have a clearly defined process to manage the project to get to a decision. The reality is that this is seldom true. Depending on what you may be selling, there is a reasonable chance the prospect has never bought anything like this before and thus don't know how. Your opportunity is to set the standard and educate them based on the best practices you see a 100 times per year. So lets assume they do have a clear process. How can you make it easier and thus make it easier to buy from you?

**Decision-Making Criteria.** Similar to the discussion above, prospects seldom have detailed decision-making criteria. In the spirit of a flanking strategy, where you are trying to change the game, you have an opportunity to educate. Would it be helpful to a project team to have a detailed decision making grid based on the best practices of 100's of decisions? That is why consultants get hired. Free of charge, you can help guide, looking like unbiased advisors.

**Industry or Competitive Influences.** Your industry can influence how the game gets played. In a previous life, an element of the buying process was always site visits from their team to one of our customers [and short-listed competitors]. We did not have choice. It was part of the sales process based on how the industry operated. We viewed it is an opportunity to differentiate and pull out all the stops. At a crucial late stage, you can potentially change the game in your favor based on how execute key sales process steps.

Remember, all things being equal, the sale experience you create will be the reason why they buy from you and stay loyal. The implication is that you are thinking differently and behaving differently from competitors.

## Summary Notes

> Sales Differentiation
> is the dominant
> factor in selection
> & loyalty.

> Most companies do
> not have a Sales
> process.

> Clients need your
> help more than
> ever before. Have a
> Vision for them.

# Exercise

We have given you a formula to re-evaluate your Sales Process and to look for areas of value creation, differentiation and innovation. The temptation is to do this in isolation or without the input of your customers. Make a list of 3-5 customers, former customers you just won or lost. Set up a call to discuss:

- Their Decision Making Criteria when they made the decision and why you really won or lost.
- How they like to buy things and how that may or may not align to how you sell things.
- Who is their best vendor and what they like about the experience of doing business with them.

# THREE
# DIY SALES LEADERS

I had the good fortune to spend the early days of my business career with one of the preeminent sales companies and sales training cultures in the world. Investment in their people (Managers and Reps) was a constant and an important point of differentiation. This was a big company and there is a theory that only large firms can invest in sales methodologies, sales training continuums and the appropriate tools. This is not true and big companies now have the exact same problems as small and medium sized businesses. This lack of investment forces Sales Leaders and to a certain extent, Sales Reps, to go into Do-It-Yourself (DIY) mode.

Why is this an issue? The primary issue is lack of consistency. In the absence of a consistent methodology, process, training, tools, etc. then Sales Leaders will rely on their own experiences, skills and self-initiative to find a way to succeed (or at least try). This does not scale very well. When only half of Reps globally achieve the desired results, you do not need to look much further than this area to understand why. Inconsistent approaches will lead to inconsistent results.

Go a little deeper and you see how this impacts hiring, from the President to the Sales Rep. Organizations seek "job ready" resources when recruiting. Partially to theoretically reduce risk and learning curves by hiring people who have done the job before and likely come from a competitor, but also because they have no way of training new hires in "how they sell".

# DIY Challenges

There are some positives in the DIY world as it pertains to creativity, innovation and doing more with less. Speed is also a factor. As the leader of a scrappy start-up, admittedly I may admire that more than most. The broader challenge is people only know what they know. Relying exclusively on their skills and experience to drive you to another level is risky.

If you are the DIY Sales Leaders you are likely bringing your previous processes, tools and potentially trusted resources with you to your new role. You need everything in your toolkit to be successful. If you are an innovator, you are also likely looking to learn and continue to raise the bar through ongoing education, reading and searching for ways to fill gaps. If you continue to do things the way you have always done them in a rapidly changing environment, then you are limiting your potential and that of the team.

*"If the only tool you have is a hammer, then every problem looks like a nail."*

Four significant factors that impact sales effectiveness (and thus results) that you may want to pay attention to are:

- Sales Organization Strategy & Structure
- Characteristics of the Sales Reps
- Role Clarity and Organization Alignment
- Sales Management Processes & Controls

# Creating Consistency

The creation of consistency will bring a level of normalcy or sanity to the Sales Leaders job. Complex sales environments have lengthy sales cycles and sizeable deals. These environments tend to create results that are a little "lumpier" and less consistent based on the nature of the beast. Creating consistent and predictable business results or outputs is a function of the inputs that consistently go into the business.

In larger organizations, the consistency issue really shows itself at the senior sales leader level. In the absence of a consistent strategy, approach, processes and tools then every person below them is leveraging their experiences and doing their own thing. This will create inconsistent results and potentially chaos. In a small organization where there is only one leader and one sales team, you are in DIY mode by default. There is nobody else. The consistency comes from the governance, processes and tools that you put in place to lead and manage the team. This helps create leverage.

As the DIY Sales Leader, some example areas of focus that create leverage are:

- A standardized hiring profile
- A governance calendar for all Sales events
- Job descriptions and Performance Tracking
- Timely compensation plans that align with performance Goals
- A documented Sales Process and Process training
- Tools that enable process, help train and increase productivity

# Alignment

If you are familiar with the "Gallup Twelve", it is well-researched set of twelve questions that become an excellent measure of employee satisfaction and engagement. The first two questions are:

1. Do you know what is expected of you at work?
2. Do you have the tools you need to do your job?

Sales is a bit more of a binary profession than most because the natural score boarding of sales results against quota give you some indication of expectations. There is obviously a lot more to it than that if a Rep or Manager is going to meet all expectations and truly be successful. This is where alignment comes into play.

Top to Bottom alignment on what is expected, how you are going to accomplish your goals and who is doing what reduces operational chaos. It also helps create an "operating rhythm" for the business. This is the leaders responsibility and cannot be delegated.

Most leaders we meet are slightly over confident on how well all of this works today. There is a material impact on Sales Effectiveness but also on morale. The consistent feedback we here from Sales Managers is that the administrative load associated with their job and the constant "fire drills", not only impact effectiveness but their ability to Lead and Coach.

Improved alignment is generally an opportunity area.

# Sales Governance

It is the leaders responsibility to set the governance processes and controls, as well as to execute them. A simple tool we often recommend is to put a Governance Calendar in place at the beginning of every year.

It establishes the operating rhythm of the Sales business. It helps with expectation setting, preparation, success measures and inspection. Consistency reduces drama and fire drills. I would recommend you get the dates in everyone's calendars during the first week of the new year and ensure all stakeholders are clear on expectations, process and tool usage.

Something as simple as the example below creates a clear operating model.

| Annual | Quarterly | Monthly | Weekly |
|---|---|---|---|
| Business Plans | Business Reviews | Communication Meeting | Team Meeting |
| Performance Reviews | Reward & Recognition Event | One-on-Ones | Deal Reviews |
| Kick-Off | | Forecast Calls | Celebrate Success |
| Strategic Planning | | Publish Inputs and Outputs | |

# Tools

We are going to spend a lot of space discussing Sales Tools in the later Chapters. The Governance Calendar sample from above has 7-8 different processes that could be enabled by Tools.

Tools help with consistency and alignment, but also with effectiveness, if used properly. If you are in DIY mode, then tools to enable process will be a very good investment to create some leverage for you.

Tools will also help Sales Leaders to be better Managers and Coaches. The key distinction here is whether you are "telling" or whether you are "asking". Managers solve problems by telling their people the answer and solving the issue. We do this too frequently because of our hectic schedules, the constraints and pressure we feel and just lack of understanding. Coaches engage in a two-way conversation to get people to understand the problem themselves and to then determine the right course of action to resolve the problem.

Well-designed Sales Tools will lead sales teams to think through the problem and their strategy on their own. It allows Managers to put their coaching hat on more frequently to ask questions to understand the teams thinking and to offer suggestions at the appropriate time. Tools have the opportunity to train and enable new behaviors.

# Selling Inside

I am not talking about the role of Inside Sales, but the complexity and challenge of selling inside your own organization. We hear from many sales leaders, a bit tongue in cheek, that this task is actually harder than selling to clients. I have lived that life.

Once again, as we preach about alignment, consistency and tools, they all work to make it easier to work both inside and outside your organization.

Think about doing a Deal Review with your CEO and CFO. In the absence of a common process or tool to guide the conversation, you are at the mercy of their style, mood and questions they want to ask. This can be like entering the proverbial lions den. Assuming you want more control and effectiveness, you can develop / guide the process and enable the process with tools.

This will help you get better outcomes and also reduce the friction points that come with many of these meetings. If other stakeholders understand your positioning and your strategy using the facts at hand, it will make it much easier to assemble the required resource investments or financial concessions required to move deals forward.

# Managing Communication

An important component of the Sales Leaders job is managing communication and expectations. As the saying goes, that could be *up, down or across* the organization. We have seen this situation several times in the past year. We are meeting with the Sales Leader and their personal view of Sales Effectiveness is far different than what our homework told us. Within 90 days, the Sales Leader goes missing in action. What happened?

Obviously every situation is different, but you could feel the disconnect in expectations between the Sales Leader and those above him/her. Was the CEO aligned to the overall Sales Strategy? Were they aligned on expectations for the sales business and required investments? How about the other functions? How about the Sales teams?

What we are clearly saying is that the majority of organizations lack some of the essential building blocks to create a highly effective sales organization. A new Sales Leader will have a honeymoon period and the latitude to make required changes. That statement does imply alignment and proper expectation setting with those around them. An existing Sales Leader will likely have a shorter leash. Our markets and competitors are getting tougher, so if organic growth is demanded, then the Sales Leader needs to have a real plan. Regardless of what the plan elements may be, then managing the communication is the Sales Leaders job.

# Summary Notes

> In the absence of consistent corporate standards, leaders become DIYer's

> Process and tools help create alignment and consistency

> Sales Leaders must own Strategic alignment and communication

# Exercise

What are the biggest areas of help, support and investment that are required for the Sales organization to meet or exceed their expectations?

If you believe in these areas and you will not be successful without them, then what is the plan (that you can lead) to move these initiatives forward?

Who are politically powerful and influential people whose support is important?

# FOUR
# THE CARROT AND STICK

Whether you are a Manager or a Rep, the use of Sales Tools can become the Carrot and Stick game. Managers need the data that the tools produce to help run the business and make decisions. Reps need to enter the data and in the list of priorities, this generally is not at the top of their list.

We are going to spend Part B of the book talking about Sales Tools that have nothing to do with CRM, but as soon as you mention Sales Tools or Software, the first thing that pops into peoples minds is CRM. This is also generally not a happy visual. This will purposefully be the shortest chapter in the book, but you cannot talk about tools without putting CRM in context.

CRM is an essential tool because of that data. Despite the mission critical nature of the information, virtually every company struggles with usage, data accuracy and getting a return on investment from their CRM system. What used to be relatively inexpensive monthly SaaS models to acquire CRM is no longer the case.

CRM vendors are adding or interfacing ancillary solutions to extend the value and stickiness of their applications. We met one such ancillary vendor who had a stand-alone value proposition that was likely better than the CRM platform. That said, their positioning was not about their business value to the sales organization, but helping drive a better return from a previous salesforce.com investment. Crazy!

The opportunity becomes to move the game from Carrot and Stick, to an aligned strategy that the sales teams understand and are enabled by tools that make everyone better.

# The CRM Story

It may seem that I am taking jabs at CRM or Sale Force Automation (SFA) tools, but I believe they fulfill a specific purpose and are (for the most part) essential. I will devote a page or two as to why this is the case and why we need this type of tool to measure, manage and coach. My critique is that organizations have acquired SFA as a quick fix to increase revenue with no sales process, implementation plan, success measures or executive sponsorship or ownership.

To learn from this challenge, new or existing tool investments will benefit from:

- Clearly defined business problems and their known impact on the organization
- Executive Sponsorship in change and investment
- Defined ownership of the tool
- Training and implementation plans
- Ongoing Processes and Controls to insure usage and compliance
- Defined Success Measurements

In the world of prevalent cloud based tools, 30 day free trials are the norm. It does allow potential customers to test tools, but it also implies all of the above are in place if you are actually going to invest in change. This is a key point because you are making process change by implementing tools. Let your process guide how you use tools - not the other way around.

# The Role of SFA

SFA tools are not new, but have certainly become more pervasive through the vast amount of vendors who provide on-line SaaS CRM. We are distinguishing SFA from broader CRM that falls into Contact Center tools and other categories. SFA has grown up from the days of on-premise Contact Management tools and focuses on a certain hierarchy of usage within most complex sales organizations.

**Territory Management**

**Account Management**

**Contact Management**

**Activity Management**

**Funnel Management**

**Opportunity Management**

**Document Management**

**Report Management**

This is a very simple structure of how this type of tool can be used effectively to help manage and measure your sales business. It begins with configuring your Sales Territories based on your Coverage Strategy to define who has what Accounts. You can collect information on those Accounts and build your database of Contacts within the Accounts and your touch points with them based on your Contact Strategy.

Your Sales Funnel tracks your Opportunities, which we will discuss separately. You can collect and create history of what has happened with the Account through a document repository. Reporting is the Holy Grail for Management as you can now measure all of the above. Reports require accurate data and are garbage-in, garbage-out. In the absence of Process & Controls, it is easy to see why 50% of companies don't use the tool well or at all, despite great intentions.

# The Rear View Mirror & The Windshield

SFA is a necessity, but lets recognize that it is the rear view mirror. It is a database of recorded inputs of what has happened in the past. The data may give you clues about the future, but it is unlikely to help you increase your Win Rate.

In Chapter 6 and 7, we are going to discuss processes and tools that are forward looking that can be become the windshield on your opportunities. Not only does this drive the consistency and alignment we seek, but also they can become a vehicle for the daily habits and common language that are outputs from these behaviours.

At a time when training is on the decline, tools can create on-the-job training for management and reps. The rear view mirror and the windshield can work together to create a very different Sales Strategy, set of behaviours and results.

# Processes and Controls

Process in the world of sales often conjures up negative connotations that go along with micro management or "process for process sake". As stated in the Introduction, the insertion of tools in the absence of process is a recipe for failure. Sales Reps will push back at the administrative burden that often gets layered on them based on the impact that it has on field time and productivity. Of course there is a reasonable balance that is required. This really is where the rubber meets the road as it pertains to Sales Tools.

Process is a critical component in defining "how you sell" as we discussed in Chapter 2. Process & Controls implies consistency, measurement and adjustment. In the absence of accurate information, candidly, we are all guessing. Process is created to drive the required Inputs (calls, proposals, demonstrations) that create the desired Outputs (prospects, orders, revenue). The Controls and Measures create the ability to understand what is working (or not) and to adjust as required on a timely basis.

With clear expectations of what is required in the way of Inputs and Outputs, then coaching becomes an overlay of the Sales Process. The best way to coach is directly to the Sales Process phases and activities with the comparative measurements that exist against known standards.

# Summary Notes

> If there is not a well-defined plan around sales tools, then save your money (and time)

> Data from sales tools is garbage in, garbage out

> Expectations, processes and controls develop operating rhythm

# Exercise

Take inventory of the various tools (software, spreadsheets, paper, etc.) that you have collected and are utilized today.

What are they the tools that add measurable value and potentially should have more focus?

What tools should be re-evaluated or abandoned? Why?

What gaps exist for us that tools could help with?

# PART B

## TRANSFORM

# FIVE

# BUILD YOUR STRATEGY

The term Sales Strategy can be used at both a macro and micro level depending on your role. At a macro level, Sales Strategy may represent the Sales Strategy for your entire business. At a micro level, it is the Strategy for a specific deal. We are going to spend time and effort to talk about both.

Regardless of your role, there are elements of Sales Strategy that we will all own. Sales are a team sport and you will need the support of others in the organization to accomplish your goals. The clearer they understand your strategy and how that supports the goals of the broader business [or that other individual], then the greater likelihood that they will engage and support your initiative.

Let me give you two different examples. You are a Sales Manager and you are revising your Coverage Strategy. You want to increase your Participation Rate in your target market. You understand the number of deals in your marketplace in any given year and you are investing in tighter sales coverage. You also need the help of the Marketing organization to create some air cover in your territories to help create increased awareness and demand when your Reps call into target accounts. Marketing will have choices to make and they need to be convinced that investing in your strategy is the best of use of finite resources.

You are a Rep and you need the support from Product Management at a critical point in a sales cycle. The prospective client perceives risk in your product roadmap and whether you are making the investments they deem as critical. You need a very busy Product Manager to get on a plane to go make the call, along with all the required prep meetings. They need to understand your deal strategy.

# Strategic Flow

This is a term I started to use a few years that denotes the flow that needs to exist between Corporate Strategy, Marketing Strategy and Sales Strategy. That is the appropriate flow or sequence [in my opinion].

The core to a Corporate Strategy is your differentiated market position that creates value for your clients and economic value for your organization. Your value proposition sits in the center of your business model. Based on your Strategy, your Marketing Strategy defines the markets you will serve and how you will go-to-market. Think about the 4 P's, not just Marcom. With your STP in place [Chapter 2], your channel choices, product strategy and pricing elements come together to frame your Marketing Strategy.

We know whom we are shooting the rifle at and our positioning is clear based on the business problem we solve and how we create differentiated value. Our Sales Strategy needs to enable our broader Corporate Strategy.

# Sales Strategy

I have seen versions of this generic visual, which we call the SPEED Model, to show some elements to consider when thinking about your Sales Strategy.

We begin by making strategic decisions about how we enable the broader strategy. Key decisions are your channel choices and the process of how you sell. With your strategic framework in place, you can lay out the plan components. Structure decisions lead to decisions about hiring, training and tools to support your resources. Goal setting if often linked directly to incentives to create alignment.

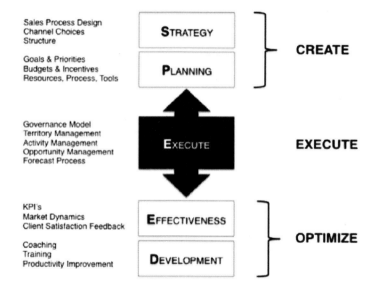

There are many elements to Execution and we only highlighted a few. The Execution arrow also goes both directions. Based on your performance results, you may need to adjust the strategy and / or the plan.

We will measure our Effectiveness through the Key Performance Indicators [KPI's] we have set for the business, our governance process, how we are performing in the competitive market as measured by market share, participation rates, win rates and other dynamics.

As we seek to optimize results and drive productivity improvements, we are looking to further Develop our people. Coaching, training and tool usage are important elements to focus on.

We look at these Sales Strategy elements as the cycle of Creation, Execution and Optimization. The continual measurement of these areas allows for rapid adjustment based on the results that we are producing.

# Resource Optimization

DIY Leaders are often forced into hiring Reps that are "just add water" and ready to go. In absence of your own methodology or way of training your staff in how you sell, then you are looking for people with industry experience, industry knowledge, product knowledge, sales experience and a database of contacts. You also get all of their bad habits that led them to you in the first place. If you have no ability to hire people and mould them in your vision of how you sell, then you hire to a specific profile that you believe has less risk and a faster productivity curve.

We see this challenge in every industry and at every level of the company. The primary job of Leaders / Managers / Coaches [the three hats you wear] is the development of your people. This creates leverage if your staff is performing at optimal levels.

There are a few components to consider as you think about the productivity of your resources. The first is the profile of people you are hiring to begin with. Most roles have job descriptions, but I am referencing the skills and attributes of the individuals that are required to be effective in the job. Inexpensive screening or testing tools are available to every company. The cost of a bad hire is a 100x more expensive than the small price to test and get real feedback on your perspective teammates. I work with one client who does this religiously. Not only is it part of the hiring profile, but also when issues arise, they go back to the profiles to get guidance of what to do from a coaching perspective to guide their next moves.

Profiling is a very good idea and if you do not know what your ideal profile is then the 3rd party providers of the tools will help you with that as well. Some simple examples of elements to consider are the attribute differences between a Hunter versus a Farmer or a Transactional sale versus a Complex Sale. The skills, behaviours and attributes required are very different.

How do you train your people on an ongoing basis? The most common type of training we see is product training or training on your internal processes. Don't get me wrong this is important stuff. The big training gap we see is at the sales process or methodology level of how you differentiate in how you sell your good and services. Small companies are reliant on the background of the sales leader to pass on their skills and knowledge or the learned experience of the reps themselves. Big companies are not that much different. Again, in the absence of a consistent way of doing things you will get very inconsistent results as everyone is doing their own thing. To optimize results, consistency through a common set of daily habits across your teams and individuals is very helpful.

In a tight expense environment where everyone is being asked to do more with less and you have no sales training budget, what can you do to improve productivity through consistency? My recommendation would be to start with the exercise to create a differentiated Sales Process. With a new Sales Process, you can develop a Tactical Playbook that supports and drives the various phases or steps. You can develop or use inexpensive Tools that support your process and create the daily habits you are looking for from your Reps and Managers. With very limited money, you have an opportunity to create a very different environment and set of results.

# Sales Management Operating System [SMOS]

A friend of mine is a senior sales leader and he uses this term, which I love [and borrowed]. This is another descriptor of Governance, but your OS should be well understood by all team members. It should be documented and key events in everyone's calendars.

Like a computer Operating System, this is the traffic cop that directs the flow and reduces chaos or drama inside the sales organization. Once in place, your OS will help set the Operating Rhythm of the sales business. One of the common complaints from other functional leaders within the business is that sales [by comparison] are less process driven and less predictable by nature. You can solve most of this perception including the predictability or visibility issue.

As the Sales Leader, this is a key part of your job. Your boss [and peers] should have clear understanding, buy-in and potentially a role in the SMOS. If you operate on an island and sales is a "black box", then you have isolated yourself and that is a dangerous place to be when times are tough. I told a story like this earlier. We had been asked by a CEO to have an introductory conversation with the VP of Sales about some of their effectiveness challenges and their focus areas for driving higher levels of organic growth. The CEO was not happy with results, but was not a sales guy and had limited visibility. The VP of Sales told us a story of puppy dogs and rainbows, nothing to see here, we got this covered. A short conversation. 90 days later the Sales VP is gone and the CEO is starting again. Results aside, the VP of Sales created no visibility into their SMOS with his peer group and paid the ultimate price.

# You Can't Delegate Strategy

We are talking about Sales Strategy and as a Sales Leader, you cannot delegate this job to Sales Operations or any other group. Your CEO cannot delegate Corporate Strategy. At the end of the day, you own all things sales and this is the foundational building block.

If you agree that you cannot delegate strategy, then where could you go for support? The simple answer is everywhere. Everywhere includes inside the company and outside. Let me illustrate:

Inside Support

- Sales Operations. Small companies may not have this but there are likely support resources you can leverage.
- Learning & Development. Who is worried about the training and engagement of employees that can help you in your mission?
- Marketing. They are your partners in crime as it pertains to awareness and demand creation. They can also support your Sales Process differentiation and client facing sales messages and campaigns.
- Finance. What? They are also your partner in reporting, forecasting and the predictability of results. They can help you with process, tools and you need them on your side, not as a foe or critic. I would bring them into the problem and make them the builder or co-owner of the solution.

These are just examples of groups you could use strategically to help you move forward, but the caveat is they need to understand your strategy.

If you are like me, you have a large network of smart friends and peers who have dealt with these problems or challenges. Go talk to them and get their guidance on how they have solved these challenges and what mistakes you should avoid based on their scars.

These things called Google and LinkedIn have created vast forums of organized information distribution and conversation sharing that gets you ideas very quickly without having to engage. Quick, easy and free, but you need to filter, because you do get what you pay for.

# Everything Is Selling

In my humble opinion, Sales is the most important activity conducted by any company because it drives all revenue. In the absence of revenue, regardless of all the cool stuff you make, it is all irrelevant. From the CEO on down, every client related activity is indirectly a selling or teaching event with clients. Every piece of information or material that marketing puts out [regardless of the channel] is a selling event.

As part of the Strategic Flow of the business, a Sales Strategy needs to connect and enable the broader strategy of the business. Remember that a key component of your competitive differentiation and why a client will be buy from you and stay loyal to you is the sales experience that you create. This will not happen by accident, so by the nature of what is required, you need a Sales Strategy before you can build your plan.

You can say the same thing internally. Everybody sells something, whether it is their ideas or themselves. The nature of risk aversion and consensus decisions forces us to be better at conveying ideas, gathering support and bringing others forward collectively.

We all get stuck in tactical mode, managing the day-to-day volume. I would encourage you to take the appropriate time to step back and think about the Strategy required to get to a different set of outcomes.

# Summary Notes

Sales Strategy is not isolated from the rest of the business

Invest in the right structure, the right resources and tools

You cannot delegate strategy

# Exercise

Strategy could be defined as the differentiated activities you undertake that create measurable value for your clients and sustainable economic value for you.

We talked about strategic flow and the connection between Corporate Strategy, Marketing Strategy and Sales Strategy. Can you connect the dots?

Invest some time to understand your Corporate Strategy, strategic goals and priorities.

Spend some similar time to understand how Marketing supports and enables your Corporate Strategy.

Given those inputs, what are critical investments that must be made in Sales Strategy?

What are the top 5 priorities?

# SIX
# CONNECT THE DOTS

We are going to spend the next couple of Chapters discussing how to leverage tools to support and enable your Sales Strategy, specifically at a deal level. Sales Tools can help create and enable process. They can drive productivity and create a framework for On-The-Job Training for both Managers and Reps. We will connect the dots on Tools to the other elements we have discussed so far.

Regardless of the Sales challenge you are focused on, chances are pretty good that you can find a tool to help you with the problem. Once again, your process needs to guide tool selection and usage, not the other way around. If you are totally void of process, then some tools will provide benchmarks that you can borrow or enhance.

One area that was listed on The Role of SFA [page 52] was Opportunity Management. This is not an area of strength for an SFA tool and this is something you would need to acquire or build yourself. There is a lot to be considered to understand and measure your positioning in a deal and to use the facts to build your deal strategy. This chapter is devoted to understanding your point in time deal positioning.

One important role that tools play in Opportunity Management is the ability to have consistent, fact-based conversations. Facts help remove emotion. For many Reps, we have never met a deal we did not like. We bid on everything. Facts help determine our true positioning so we both build timely Action Plans and make the appropriate strategic decisions.

# Where Am I?

One of the challenges we have in complex pursuits [or pursuits in general] is that it is difficult to truly gauge where we are and how we are positioned. The impact can be profound. As we have already discussed, complexity is growing and the competitive environment is intensifying. Most of us have funnels that are smaller than we would like and thus when opportunities come our way, it is difficult for us to be objective about our chance of being successful. Remember, more than 50% of deals go to "No Decisions" or staying with the status quo. This puts the onus on us to pick the right deals to compete in. Business Leaders will talk about cost of sale or deploying their valuable resources against the right deals. Even for Reps, the most valuable resource you have is your time, so use it wisely.

Tools can help create a consistent conversation and ask the right questions about the deal elements to give us a truer, objective assessment of where we really are. They will help eliminate emotion. The tools may tell you to get out of the deal, but that is not really the point. The point is about helping you decide what to do next from a decision making and action planning perspective. This is the windshield that we referenced back in Chapter 4.

You can call this Opportunity Management or Deal Reviews, but at the highest level there are core things we need to understand about the opportunity. Given clients propensity for the status quo, how likely are they to make change? Given your sweet spot is this the type of opportunity you should be competing in? Can you differentiate your value story given what the client is trying to accomplish and how they will judge you? Can we Win?

These are the core questions that we will answer separately. Sales are like pro sports; you are in the game of winning. There are no trophies or moral victories for second place. If tools can help you be better, compete better, be more strategic and help you win, then we should embrace the opportunity. As you are likely gathering, I am not talking about recording data about what happened three calls ago. This is the forward-looking windshield.

This is all about us thinking differently and being more strategic within our opportunities.

# Are They Really Making Change?

I will often ask Sales Teams the question about the "Compelling Event" that is leading clients to make change. A response I hear all the time is their contract is expiring. On a scale of 1-10 [10 being high] of compelling events, in our current world a contract expiry is about a 2. They do not need to make change and the easiest path is a renewal because of switching costs, effort, risk and a bunch of other factors. The greatest 10 in business history was Y2K. It drove trillions of dollars of business decisions because the world was theoretically coming to an end if you did not do certain things by a very exact moment in time.

If we are going to invest in a pursuit, the first thing we need to understand is the likelihood they are actually going to make change. In a previous life we used the age of the CEO as a key indicator of change. Is the organization engaged in a tire kicking exercise to see what is out there and get a better price from the current vendor or a true investment in change? There are many questions we would encourage you to consider.

What is the business problem they are trying to resolve and how does that connect to their business goals?

What is the evidence that the problem exists?

Have they quantified the impact of the problem or can you help them do that?

This may not be new, so what has prevented them from solving this problem previously and will it stop them again?

How does the problem connect to the advancement of their mission or goals?

Have they allocated the appropriate cash, time and resources to solve this problem?

As with all the questions we may pose, you may not know the answer. Depending on where you are in the sales / buying process, this creates different risks and concerns. If you are on call #1, then you are unlikely to know, but that does lead you to action items and a plan.

If you are late in a deal and you don't know, then that is a totally different matter and likely does not position you well.

# Should You Invest?

In any pursuit you are making investments and decisions. You are investing the time of many valuable resources and likely real dollars as well on travel and other hard dollar costs. The decision, given your likelihood of being successful, is whether this is a deal you should invest in or not. All deals are not created equal based on various factors that are important to you. If you modelled your wins you will find common themes that lead you to a certain sweet spot that increases your likelihood of success.

More questions for you to consider.

What is the deal size [compared to your average] and what is the future revenue potential?

What is the potential margin?

What is the risk to you? Clients are trying to transfer risk through contract terms to their vendors. You have contractual risk, execution risk, financial risk and other risks to consider.

How does this match up to your target market and is this a coveted new hill? Is it a strategic win that will lead you to other places?

What do we know about how we will be judged and does that line up with our strengths?

What do we know about the client's process and the players that will show up? Does that work in our favour or against us?

Do we have access to the key stakeholders or are we the kids with our noses pressed against the glass?

Our ability to educate clients and to get them thinking differently is impacted by access, credibility and candidly, how we tell our story.

We are again looking for unemotional clues as to whether we should invest our valuable and expensive resources. Tools can play the role to help you ask the right questions at the right time and to help guide your action plans.

# Can We Truly Differentiate?

I am a believer that there are always ways to differentiate. The caveat is our ability to think differently as a starting point, to be able get clients thinking differently and to make our points of differentiation a critical element of the decision process. This is real work and requires a strategic approach to our commercial conversations.

I learned some important concepts about a Value Proposition in my time at Kellogg [business school - not cereal company]. The theory is there are three sides to a value proposition. In the end, all three sides equate back to the price you will pay in a monetary unit for the quality of the good or service.

The three sides of the Value Proposition are:

*Functional / Technical Value.* The reference is to the feature or function and technical benefits a client will receive. This could also be about process and other key elements that may influence the opinion of who has the better mousetrap.

*Economic Value.* This is not just price, but more ROI, cost avoidance, and other areas that can create economic return.

*Psychological Value.* This has been proven to be the most powerful of three and the most difficult to copy by competitors. We make decisions using emotion and subjective judgement every day. Brand momentum, relationships, trust, service levels, cultural fit, strategic fit and other decision making factors are all psychological.

If you were to measure your deal positioning against these 3 value attributes against known competitors, where do you think you stand?

How do these line up against stated decision-making criteria?

Can you get clients thinking different about the criteria that they should be using if they are too narrow?

Can you measure the impact that your solution will have on their business goals or priorities?

How does the level of your client relationships stack up against known competitors?

What we have found when we talk about the value you create is that you may be speaking a different language than your clients. Think about one of your products. What are three ways that product / service creates value for clients? Write it down. Now think about how that should translate into the language your customer actually speaks based on what they care about. Write down the value in your clients' language in the column next to your language. They are likely very different because your column is likely focused on the features of the product and the client is focused on the business outcome they hope to achieve.

# Can We Win?

This is what it is all about. Moral victories and learning opportunities are what we may take from defeat, but if we are going to compete, then we are there to Win. All deals are not created equal based on your chances of success.

We need to understand our positioning and our strategy to gain clarity on whether we can win the day.

How did we get involved in the deal? Did we create it or did we get invited? These are very different things.

Where do we think we are positioned? Are we ahead or behind? If you are not the incumbent and got invited to the party, whether you know it or not, you are likely way behind.

Do you have history with this account or with people on the client team? How about in deals this size or in this market? History helps predict the future.

Do we actually have a strategy or are we guessing?

Price will always be a factor. Are we able to model our price to win based on our positioning?

The incumbent vendor always has "incumbent advantages". Even if there are challenges, between switching costs, price discounts, familiarity and relationships, incumbents can create unique leverage. If you were the incumbent, what would you do?

What is your reputation and / or credibility with this client and this market? Your answer may change your tactics.

What will this pursuit require in the way of your time and resources? Is this only the "A Team" and all of their time? What else is impacted by your resourcing decisions or choices?

WOW is one of my favourite words in the English language. It is normally a positive, spontaneous response to an event. We like to try and create or plan WOW moments in a pursuit. What can you do to blow the client away that could potentially change the game in your favour?

When you pull all of these elements together, we are trying to get a clear and quantifiable assessment of our current positioning. This could be a score, but that score only gives us another data point that impacts our action planning and decision-making.

# A Point In Time

You can test all of these elements at various points in a pursuit. If you just got involved in the deal, you would expect to have more questions than answers and thus you will build an action plan to go gather more information to support decision-making. You may also have enough info based on what you don't know and how the client is responding to you to tell you to get out of this deal now.

If the deal is further advanced and you still have many unanswered questions, then you likely have a positioning challenge. Tools, through consistency, help bring these challenges to the surface.

If you believe you are nearing the finish line, you should have strategic clarity and understand your positioning very well. You should also understand the clients' process to get to consensus.

One of the challenges sales leaders own, that impacts other functions in the business, is the predictability of sales results. Sales is more art than science and as much as we would like to think we control our deals, those darn clients actually have the control. This creates predictability challenges that we have already referenced. A consistent way of reviewing, discussing and measuring our opportunities helps create improved predictability.

# Action Planning

I have been in the lions den enough times reviewing deals [or been the lion] to say that the real productivity that comes from the exercise comes from the resulting Action Plans and the ability to make unemotional decisions. I will discuss these separately.

Strategy is about choice. Investing your money and valuable resources is about choice. Using the information we have at our disposal to build an Action Plan at that Point In Time creates alignment on the team and movement. You will gather again to review actions and will either develop new actions or use progress [or not] to make other decisions.

This is more of a tactical exercise to get the information required to help make more strategic decisions. That is OK, it needs to be done. In the absence of information, you and your team are GUESSING. Guessing, strategy and investment are not words that go together.

# Decision Making

There are many decisions that need to be made on an ongoing basis as part of a pursuit process. The first decision and now an ongoing decision is to pursue or not to pursue. There are several elements we need to consider. Will the client actually make change? If we think not, we are consuming valuable time and resources on the hope of creating goodwill for the future. Data would suggest because of risk aversion, increased governance and the impact of consensus decision-making on the client side, there is a better than 50% chance they will do nothing. Tools can help you decipher the code.

Can you differentiate and win? If you have convinced yourself to pursue, then it is likely because you like your chances to compete and win. This forces strategic decisions about how you will compete or differentiate. It also forces tactical decisions about pricing, travel, resource allocation and the plays from the tactical playbook you want to run. All of the above use resources and energy.

Is this the best use of our valuable resources? Given the other conflicting priorities, the team and money required, if this were your money would you make this bet? We talked previously about the role of information in decision-making, otherwise we are guessing. Tools can help provide a compass in our deals that get overlaid with our "gut feel" or experience.

# Summary Notes

Tools create leverage

Everybody needs a deal compass

Guessing and Strategy Don't Go Together Well

# Exercise

Whether you are a Manager or a Rep, we all require a compass or common set of questions that need to be answered on each deal. I gave you some categories and ideas.

You may have a tool and framework that you or your company use today.

Based on some new ideas, what remodeling would you do to your existing tool? If you were to create your own tool, what would you to include to raise your thinking and the quality of internal conversations?

Remodel or Design your own simple tool.

Test your new tool with your peers, colleagues or your boss.

# SEVEN
# GETTING MORE INK

The ink reference is obviously not about your tattoo preferences, but to getting more ink on paper or the metaphorical contract signing of new deals. If this is the end game from a more effective and transformed sales organization, then what are the key levers we can pull?

We talked about Sales Strategy in the macro and micro sense of the term. There are a lot of components to consider in the macro definition of a Sales Strategy that defines how this will work at a company level. If this works well, then the alignment, consistency and well-considered process / people /tool investments should contribute to more ink.

We are talking about the micro definition or deal level Sales Strategy. You are now in the thick of the battle and you will be using client information, market information, competitive information and your areas of value differentiation to create your plan. As the great philosopher, Mike Tyson says: "Everyone has a strategy until they get punched in the face!" You should expect to continually adjust.

The use of tools and information once again helps you make choices and better decisions. We know where we are positioned and we are creating our Deal Strategy.

# The Cast of Characters

If we need better information about the client and the opportunity to shape our strategy then a good starting point is to think about the cast of people who will be showing up on the client side of the opportunity. Lets assume for the sake of this discussion that we are ones that created the opportunity with the client.

What we know is that there will likely be 5 or more people or potentially groups of people involved in the opportunity. Complexity and consensus almost guarantee this fact. Can we identify who they are or could likely be?

We like to understand and track several different variables against the individuals or groups on the client side that are involved in the process. Start with the simple stuff. What functions of the business will be impacted and will need to be involved in the decision process? IT, Operations, Finance, Marketing, HR, and Sales are examples of groups that may get invited for their perspective because they are impacted by the proposed change. Within each of these functions, there could be a cast of characters. Use IT as an example, given what the solution and impact may be. CIO, VP of IT, IT Manager, Development, Architects, Engineers are groups and roles within IT. They all have different interests, perspectives and biases.

They may get invited or you may want them invited. Based on how you create value and differentiate, a key part of your strategy may be to bring in other stakeholders who can mobilize change and increase your chance of success.

# Roles

Different than their job title, people may be asked to play specific roles in the buying process. Some examples could include:

**Authorizer**. Either because of the internal process and thus who needs to sign, someone could be an Authorizer because of their title or because they actually own the P&L or line of business.

**Influencer**. In a world of consensus, more influencers are being invited from all functions. These could be people with political sway, who can either get things done or stop things from happening all together. They could also be 3rd parties that get brought in to provide context and reduce risk.

**Justifier**. People may be part of the process because they authorize the business case or ROI from a financial perspective. They also may be Subject Matter Experts that justify or validate the functional solution.

**Operators**. Think about IT buying a solution for Sales. I would hope it would actually work the other way around, where sales is buying something that IT supports, but we see all kinds of crazy things out there. In this case, the Sales Leaders are the functional owners that should have a loud voice, as they there are also the users of the solution.

We are proponents of trying to understand the various people and roles they will play. We often underestimate the people involved and their motivations. Think about a deal you lost because of people who either stopped the deal or voted for a competitor and you did not know they existed [until after the loss].

History lessons are helpful to understand future behavior. The clients buying process is changing and getting more complex. This is a great opportunity to understand [through conversation] how decisions like this get made and who on the client side is likely to get involved based on similar recent decisions.

# Relationships

In the simplest world, we need to understand whether people in the cast are friends or foes. There are many elements to consider here. What is their history with you and your company? What is their history or investment in the incumbent relationship? How will change impact them directly? Is the solution good for their group and does it help the business achieve their goals?

You have all heard the various sales terms like Coach or Fox to describe someone working on the inside to help you out. The implication here is that there are personal or corporate wins involved in them implementing your solution. Data would suggest that these two things are no longer created equal. According to CEB, people seeking personal wins are unlikely to be able to mobilize change because of lack of either political will or personal credibility. People seeking corporate wins have a much greater chance of influencing change. Finding a coach is still possible, but the recommended tactic is to nurture and develop people who can help lead change because of the strength of the business case for change and the outcome for the client organization.

We will have some supporters, some detractors and some people that are neutral. We need to pay attention to them because depending on what happens next in the buying process, they are going to go one direction or the others.

We may also have known stealth adversaries. They may be very transparent or they may be hidden and thus your insiders will need to identify them. Their reasons may not be personal; they may just be committed to the status quo. Don't want to change, too much to do, too much perceived risk are all examples. Coming from the technology world, I get to see IT "holy wars" all the time. If someone has invested their entire career in being an Oracle Database expert [insert Microsoft, IBM, Cisco or any other name here], then anything that threatens what they have spent their career doing is likely a firm "no" regardless of the organizational impact.

I have lost deals in my career where we underestimated the groups desire to do anything with our Partners and they voted for any solution that would prevent that from happening. I have lost deals because of the influence of small, low level groups [bank tellers] because they did not like the software workflow compared to how they do it today. I have lost deals because we underestimated peoples' commitment to the status quo even after a massive investment of their time and money.

What we lacked in these scenarios was visibility and tactics of how to effectively deal with our adversaries. In every situation, as the leader, this was my fault.

# Power Grid

We are identifying people, functions, roles and relationships. Within the client organization they are not all created equal. Power is not evenly distributed across the grid. Understanding power can only be uncovered through questions and human conversation. You will not find this information on their LinkedIn profile.

Enclosed are a few things to consider when thinking about power sources:

Who owns the direction of the Business Unit you are selling to?

Who owns the P&L?

Whose endorsement is required for this type or scale of project?

Who has influence that is disproportionate to their job title?

Who will evaluate and approve the financial justification?

Who is the Subject Matter Expert [SME] who will be consulted on the solution?

Who owns a successful implementation?

Who represents the users?

Who can influence the decision-making factors of how you are being judged?

Who are the other functional leaders who will be directly impacted by this project?

Power is not equally distributed and you will act differently at a tactical level based on whom you know and what you know.

# Value

Value is like the words Partner or Solution in the world of business. They are over used and misunderstood. When I reference value, I am going back the value proposition definition. We can define and measure value or quality in the terms that are important to the customer based on how they are going to judge us.

The question is this:

Can we quantify the value to them [company or individual] of implementing our solution over the various alternatives that exist [including the status quo]?

Do we know what is in it for them to buy from you? Given the various mandates, interests and perspectives, there will not just be one answer to this question. It is going to be different by function and role. You can aggregate value at the highest or organization level, which will quantify the business outcome for the client. If you can help them reduce cost by 15% or decrease time-to-market by 30%, despite the direct impact on their group, they may support the greater cause.

We generally see an opportunity for sales teams to do a much better job in building the value story for their clients. This requires process and skills on our side. It also requires access and support from the client. If clients deny these critical elements, this is a good test of their commitment to change, but is also a good test to understand your positioning.

# Measuring Differentiation

When clients are making decisions they will often create scoring systems or scorecards to measure vendors against the important criteria by which they are being judged. We have created tools to emulate the same process the client is going to go through that can be used by vendors. There are several uses and benefits.

The first usage or benefit starts with a better understanding of the clients' decision-making criteria. Even if they stated this in the RFP, it would not be an appropriate level of detail to really help you. There is a good chance that the client has also not really considered this at the appropriate level either, specifically early in their process. Our job is to understand and to potentially educate the client, based on best practices that other clients have utilized. We may want to influence decision criteria. For us to educate and influence, we need a better understanding of the clients' process and perspective.

Working with one of our clients, we created a Vendor Scorecard that their sales teams use for this exact purpose. When discussing decision criteria with their prospective customers, they will often get generic answers because their client has no process. The sales teams offer, based on the fact that they do this hundreds of times a year and have aggregated the best client processes, is to give the prospective client a scorecard template to utilize. Even if the client does not use the whole thing, you have likely planted 4-5 new things to consider that they had not previously. They also likely align to your unique value.

The second usage or benefit is to get feedback and to either further educate or adjust your strategy. If you have modeled how you believe you are being judged and where you think you are positioned against known competitors, you could show this to client stakeholders to get feedback. This should create a learning opportunity for them as well, but you can get feedback on criteria, positioning, competitors and other valuable components of the opportunity.

You can test this with multiple people on the client side to verify and validate. Again, power is not evenly distributed, nor is knowledge.

Being able to measure differentiation is one thing, being able to impact it is quite another. At least if you understand, you have the ability to adjust tactically. The learning will also be valuable to future pursuits as the same challenge will likely exist and you will adjust your positioning proactively.

# Deal Strategy

There are some traditional terms and theories around deal strategy that come from the military. Going all the way back to Sun Tzu [Chinese military general, strategist, and philosopher] and The Art of War, which has been adjusted and adapted for the world of business many times. I will use some of those terms for competitive strategy to illustrate a point. The strategic terms are interesting, but it is the supporting tactical plan that leads you forward.

If you ask Sales Reps what their strategy is on a deal, you are going to get an interesting array of answers. From very articulate, to we are going to try our best, to we will follow the process that has been laid out in front of us, you will hear every conceivable answer.

There is an opportunity to create common strategic language and alignment within our sales teams. I will use the Sun Tzu terms as examples of Strategy and the implications for sales teams.

**Frontal Strategy**. It is implied that you have overwhelming superiority in key areas. You will leverage those attributes through speed and force. This is seldom the case in business, but this is the strategy most reps do in most deals. Just plunge forward headfirst. This is the strategy the University of Alabama football team will deploy against Charleston Southern [no, I am not making up the name of the school they are actually playing in their second last 2015 game]. Alabama always schedules what amounts to an exhibition game to rest starters but stay sharp the week before their huge inter-state rivalry game against Auburn. They will deploy a Frontal Strategy and drive it straight at their inferior opponent.

**Flanking Strategy**. You are seeking to change the game or decision criteria to create advantage based on your unique Value. If you are Charleston Southern, you will be armed with every trick play you can muster and will try and get Alabama to play your game. Good luck with that, but it is your best shot. In business terms, think about trying to re-educate the client if you show up late to the game. If you are behind and not well positioned, you need to change the game or get out of the game.

**Fragmentation Strategy**. Your Value Proposition does not enable advantage for the prospects entire need, but you do have superiority for a portion. This is an interesting strategic choice in the world of the status quo. If you don't think you can win the big game or you don't think they will make change, then a fragmentation play allows the client to make a "small bet" and move forward. This can be very powerful.

**Stall.** Your are behind or came in late. You need value-based reasons for the prospect to delay the buying decision, such as game changing new product you are launching. You need credibility, relationships and a compelling value promise to execute this play.

Disengagement and getting out of the deal is also a strategy.

These are all traditional examples of *offensive* strategies. There are also similar *defensive* strategies. If you ask a Sales Rep what their strategy is and they say Fragmentation Strategy, you just set up a way more interesting conversation. It implies strategic and positioning understanding. It is also implies there is a tactical plan.

# Tactical Plans

You have selected a Strategy because you believe this choice will give you the greatest chance of success. This is an obvious Manager question. What is your rationale that lead you to believe this is our best strategic choice? The next obvious question relates to the tactical plan you will deploy to execute your strategy.

I will tell you a personal story based on our software strategy. In general, we are competing against doing nothing or the status quo. We are not looking to commit clients to multi-year deals for tools they won't use. We are trying to get them to transform their sales results by developing a much better Sales Strategy. Tools play an important role. As a start-up, you are dealing with criteria that relate to risk [perceived vendor risk, risk of change, financial risk] and the need to make change. Again, just buying a tool in the absence of a process and commitment from all stakeholders to change is a total waste of money. We want to leverage this fact.

We will often deploy a Flanking Strategy. We want to set the stage based on how we sell, price, contract and deploy the software to clearly differentiate from competitors. We want to change the game and the criteria. We are not always successful, but we are also very selective.

Complex Sales are a team sport and if the team is building the Tactical Plan for a deal, you will also build a repository of successful tactics that you can use over and over again. I will use the terms alignment and consistency one more time to reinforce the point.

# Price To Win

This is another very common Manager or CEO / CFO question. What do you think our Price to Win is? Given the competitive dynamics, economic pressures and other factors, what is going to be required to Win the day? This is a very hard question, but there are always clues to help you.

Most solutions are complex enough that it is not just one price of a component, product or service. There could be 5 or 50 pieces to the puzzle that aggregate into your *price*. You will build enough competitive knowledge over time to understand the different approach to pricing that your competitors take. You will also understand where they are higher or lower. They may bundle or give things away that you don't.

Your Price To Win is directly correlated to the unique value you [or your competitors] have either created or added. If the perception is that your competitor has greater quality [newer product, better service, lower risk, higher trust, clearer roadmap, etc.] then the client will pay a higher price. In this scenario, your Price To Win will need to be considerably south of your competitor unless you can change those perceptions.

If you believe you have "value adds" that the client acknowledges as such, then we need to be able to quantify the value. You may have received the head nod when you said it to one of the stakeholders. That is nice, but the real value is when they add it to the scorecard based on the quantifiable difference of what you bring to the table that others do not.

# Strategic Theme

My last point in this section may sound a little hokey as a tactic, but I have seen this be incredibly powerful as a point of differentiation. If you have a Strategy, it should link to the value you create for the client and how you will make them better. To be clear, it is all about the client.

What I am encouraging you to consider is how you may *theme* your pursuit. A theme will create strategic clarity for your team and has an opportunity to set you apart from your competitors. It will show the client that you care, you are paying attention and that you are different.

In a past life, we sold enterprise software to Financial Institutions. This is mission critical stuff that is their database and transaction-processing engine. It is the most important technology they possess. As you can imagine, the Bank may make change every 20+ years because of the complexity, risk, cost and other factors. These are 12+ months long, very complex sales cycles that often have 3rd party consultants that run the RFP's. We would usually theme the big pursuits.

Based on the problem the client was trying to resolve, why they were making change, the outcome we were hoping to accomplish and how we believed we differentiated, we would brainstorm a theme. Once we had a theme, we would bring it to life. We would normally introduce our theme at a large client presentation or event and couple it with t-shirts, coffee mugs, buttons and other visuals to show that we got it. You could see quickly if the theme resonated and whether we hit the mark.

As we went forward, the client would start using our language and reinforce the theme. It created energy and fun on our team and often the exact same thing with prospective clients. The cost was irrelevant in the big scheme of things, but we had already made the strategic decision to pursue, so this was the right type of deal to invest in.

If you have made the decision to pursue, then you should double down your bets and pull out all the stops. A Theme is just one way of doing that to further differentiate you and your brand.

# Summary Notes

Sales is the business of winning

You can measure differentiation

We need REAL deal strategies

# Exercise

Develop your own version of the deal scorecard that clients may be using to measure you against known competitors. Build a detailed grid or table.

On the top or X-axis, name yourself and your most common 2-3 competitors. Create a left side column that details the Factors of Competition that by which you are commonly judged. Price, Feature/Functions, Service, Risk, Cultural Fit, are all examples. As stated earlier, you need more detail in each Factor [as do your clients] to be able to judge or create differentiation. Create the detail below each Factor of Competition.

Now rate yourself against your competitors. 1-10 or whatever scales you deem appropriate. Where do you think you are positioned?

Your natural biases would have come though both in your Factor categories and your rating. That is OK. Specifically in the Factors column it will give you clues to how you differentiate and critical Factors you need clients to consider when making decisions.

Test this with your peers.

# EIGHT
# EXECUTE

You have a strategy, you have a plan, you have process, you have skilled resources, you have your operating system, you have tools and now it is time execute transformation. Sales Leaders are *THE* critical linkage point between strategy and execution. If they are not leading the transformation, then you are wasting a lot of time and money. Despite good intentions, unfortunately I get to see a lot of organizations doing exactly that.

If you lacked some of the required elements previously, execution will feel different as you execute a plan consistently across an aligned sales organization. It does not make the task any easier, but it will feel different. I would encourage you to look for some quick wins and to build momentum quickly. Over communicate what is happening, measure all your inputs and outputs so that you can adjust in real time.

I would encourage the creation of an Execution Plan. Goal setting is the easy part. Execution can be Hard with a capital H. This is the exercise that I outline at the end of the Chapter.

*"A goal without a plan is a dream."*

# Chaos and Drama

Think about times in your career when you felt chaos in the work environment and the events that surrounded the work always created too much drama. Especially when things are not going as planned, chaos and drama are far to common. Chaos and drama can be outputs of the lack of a plan and the lack of alignment. I worked in an environment where it almost felt desperate and the corresponding direction changed daily [or so it felt]. I would have called it strategy versus direction, but part of the challenge was a lack of strategy.

Time pressures, financial pressures, Board pressures can all create stress points for senior management that are felt all the way through the organization. This can help create the required urgency but almost certainly create chaos. This impacts senior managements reputation. If 95% of staff does not understand the strategy of the business, then all they get to see is chaos with very limited understanding.

A strategy and a well-communicated execution plan will go a long way. For the stakeholders in the execution plan, role clarity, clear expectations and having the tools to do their job help reduce the chaotic feel and also help you to develop rhythm.

# Daily Habits

A key element of execution is instilling the daily habits in all stakeholders as a key element of transformation or change. The age-old data point is that it takes 21 days to create a new habit. Whether we are talking about going to the gym, diet or our work habits, it takes time and repetition to get different results.

Tools can play a tremendously important role in developing daily habits. As Managers, given the breadth of responsibilities and the span of your team, you likely spend less than 5% of your time with any given person over the course of a year. You need to create leverage, so that your teammates are developing while you are not with them. Once again, tools can play an important role as asking the right questions and driving the right process in your absence.

Chances are pretty high that if you have CRM compliance then through the "carrot and stick", you have forced daily disciplines around CRM usage. Any new habit or tool adoption will likely require some similar coercion.

# OJT

*"If you want to teach people a new way of thinking, don't bother trying to teach them. Instead, give them a tool, the use of which will teach them a new way of thinking."*

-Richard Buckminster Fuller

This quote that we threw in at the beginning of the book is very appropriate. We do want Reps and Managers to think different and we believe tools create a great opportunity to shape new perspectives through On-The-Job Training [OJT]. We have seen this in action with our clients.

The world of sales training is an interesting place these days. Investments have been declining and the focus is often on less expensive eLearning modules. That can work well with product training but less so with sales strategy.

If you have sales tools that can repeatedly model your sales strategy and create the daily habits and disciplines, then you can create leverage and accelerate consistent execution. If your Managers are driving a similar process that the tools model and promote, once again you begin to create consistency and alignment.

You also develop a common language across the business from the CEO on down. If all the functions understand and are aligned in strategy and execution, the whole business feels more like a team because you are speaking the same language.

# ROI

How would you measure the *return on investment* from incorporating new tools [or training] within the sales business? There are some common metrics like Win Rate that are obvious, but let me give another metric to consider that relates to Cost of Sale.

Have you ever calculated the cost to pursue an opportunity? I have seen estimates as high as 10% of the deal size as a cost to pursue in long, complex deals. Let me give you a simple formula, which is the cost of a meeting. An RFP comes in the door for a major piece of business. Your first decision is to bid or not to bid. The people involved in the decision meetings could be:

*CEO or GM*
*SVP of Sales*
*Sales Manager*
*Sales Rep*
*Solution Consultant*
*RFP Manager*

Start by guessing the fully loaded compensation for those people, divide by 220 working days in a year and 8 hours in a day. You now have an hourly cost for that meeting. This is a $400-$500 per hour meeting. You can access tools that can help you drive that meeting, build your plan and help you unemotionally make decisions that cost less in a year than the cost of that one-hour meeting.

If tools can help you with your Win Rate, then this math is easy and compelling. What is your current Win Rate? What do you think it could be? Take that delta and multiple that number by your average deal size, average deal margin % and the number of deals this represents in a year.

To illustrate:

Current Win Rate = 20%
Desired Win Rate = 30%
Average Deal Size = $50,000 Total Contract Value
Average Gross Margin = 45%
Number of Deals Participated In Last Year = 200

The profit opportunity from winning 10% more often is $450,000 per year. How much would you invest to have an opportunity to increase profit by $450,000 annually?

# Measure

Transformational change will have a number of success measurements tied to the initiative. Sales is a lot like sports, so measuring high level success is pretty easy. Some sample metrics could include:

Sales $
Total Contract Value
Sales Units
Cost of Sale
Gross Margin
Participation Rate
Win Rate
Cross-Sales Penetration
Market Share
Average Deal Size
Sales Cycle Length
Number of Managers Achieving Quota
Number of Reps Achieving Quota

Depending on your industry and what you measure today, you could easily add another 5-10. Less is likely more, but determine the critical metrics that signal both momentum and success. Some will be Trailing Indicators [Sales] and some will be Leading Indicators [Sales Funnel Size].

Determine your baseline of what you achieved in the past as a norm, set your goals and measure on the appropriate cadence for your business. That could be daily, weekly, monthly or quarterly. The further apart the measurement points, then it makes adjustment less timely and potentially too late to make a difference.

# Adjust

Adjustment will continually be required. This could be to strategic elements, planning, execution and tactical items like pricing or tool usage. Your ability to adjust in a timely fashion using facts to guide decisions relates directly to processes and controls. If you understand what should be happening and what you expect, you can adjust on the fly.

There is a simple rule that you can put in place that we call "No Guessing". You do not want to be in a position where you are making moves because of poor results, but you are guessing as to whether they are the right moves based on the unknown root causes of the problem. You need facts to support your decisions.

Your ability to rapidly adjust within deals follows the same principle. If you have the process and tools to know where you are in deals, then you dramatically increase your chances of being in the right deals and your win rate in the fights you choose to have.

# Operating Rhythm

We have used this term to describe the cadence of the business with a clear Sales Strategy and a well-defined Operating System. The warning is that like other habits, it will likely take you 90 days or more to really establish the new rhythm of the sales business. You will feel it. If you are the architect, be open minded to make change based on the feedback from the team, assumingly you do not compromise on strategic intent.

You are establishing a culture of high accountability as part of the Operating Rhythm. If everyone understands their role, their expectations and they have the required tools, then we are holding all stakeholders to a higher accountability standard. Transformation cannot be successful without accountability for results or outcomes.

# Summary Notes

New Strategy execution
needs New Habits

On-the-Job Training is a
powerful lever

Measure and Adjust
Frequently

# Exercise

Execution requires a plan. The good news is you are committed to making change and you have a Strategy. Think of this transformational journey like a project.

What are the core elements of the project?

What are the detailed activities that enable the core elements or phases?

What is the timing of each element or phase?

What are the dependencies and risks?

What help and support is required?

Build a project plan.

# CONCLUSION

# Think Different

When I am speaking with larger groups about the changing sales environment, the greatest challenge and opportunity are to get clients thinking differently about their current situation. If we are going to get our clients to think different, who needs to think different first?

You likely just said "Us" inside your head.

The nature of transformational work is that it forces people to think different about the problem, which leads to different and more innovative solutions to solve the problem. The same holds true for sales pursuits. If we think different about the opportunity, we will actually behave different, we will sound different in front of the client team and there is a pretty good chance we will actually be treated different by the client.

Tools can play an important role to guide our thinking and force us to answer or ask ourselves questions that we would not otherwise. We use Strategy Tools with clients that force them to think very differently about their Corporate Strategy in a similar way that we use Sales Tools.

# Creating Leverage

Whether you are an Executive, Sales Leader, Manager or Rep, we all need to create leverage within our work. Transformation exercises are not for the faint of heart and are usually intended to get an organization from a defined point A to point B. *A different set of activities will create a different set of outcomes.* By the nature of that last sentence, the work is strategic because of the choices that need to be made.

Over the course of the almost 30 years that I have been playing the business game, you learn from as many mistakes as victories. You become battle-hardened and develop your own perspectives and approaches. This book is a collection of ideas, blogs, articles, processes and tools that we have developed, used or borrowed from smarter people over the many years. Hopefully, you can use 1-2 of the suggestions or ideas to help you create some leverage in your world.

The context of leverage is that you cannot do it yourself and you need to be able to get more from the resources, processes, tools and technology around you to get a different outcome.

# Inspiration Speed

We all have ideas and they can have a reasonably long shelf life. Inspiration is like milk and it can expire. If you are looking to drive change and you are inspired to action, do not wait two months to do it. The inspiration is gone and inspiration has a productivity multiplier. Think speed.

For many companies we see, they have a much greater potential for revenue growth [and the company] than they may be able to visualize. Can you inspire your group or your organization to take action to get you different results? Let me leave you with a thought from another author that sums up the inspiration opportunity and the risk:

*"Great companies don't hire skilled people and motivate them, they hire already motivated people and inspire them. Unless you give motivated people something to believe in, something more than their job to work toward, they will motivate themselves to find a new job and you will be stuck with whatever's left."*

For most of us, we can be more strategic, we can plan better, leverage our resources and be better communicators regardless of our role.

Thanks for reading our little book and hopefully we have inspired you to transform and take action [and given you a few tools to help you in your journey].

Cheers.

# RESOURCES

**INK Sales Strategy Software**
www.inksoftware.com

**Our Blog**
www.forceink.com/blog

**Sales Effectiveness Survey**
www.forceink.com/sales-effectivness-quiz

**Twitter**
@Force_Ink

# ACKNOWLEDGEMENTS

I would like to thank my wife Camille for her daily inspiration and joy. She drives the family energy for our sons and myself. This book is a collection of ideas from the experiences you collect over a lifetime and all the great people that you have learned from over the years.

I will acknowledge my friends at CEB for their insights and thought leadership in many areas. The transformative work we do together challenges my thinking and my desire to continually improve my craft.

Finally, here a list of people who have influenced my thinking [whom I know or wish I did]:

| | |
|---|---|
| Jimmy Buffett | Tom Russell |
| Marcus Buckingham | Doug Lord |
| Steve Jobs | Cam Ubell |
| Tom Peters | Jim Doherty |
| Tony Robbins | Al Varney |
| Steven Covey | Will Harris |
| Malcolm Gladwell | Willie Goddard |
| George McGourty | Bob Courteau |
| Elliott Lipsey | David Clark |
| Ryan Sawatzky | Bruce Derraugh |
| Dave Bowman | Martin Fairn |
| Paul Koziarz | James Ferguson |
| Ernie Philip | Ed Seagram |
| Steve Powless | John Dowd |

Blair Goulet is an entrepreneur and transformational strategist. He is the Co-Founder and Managing Partner of Force Inc. and their INK Sales Strategy Software. He regularly works Fortune 500 organizations on transformation projects to further differentiate their brand and drive organic growth, often in partnership with CEB. The same business challenges exist in clients they support across the Fortune 500, 5000 or Fortune 5M.

He is a former President of Open Solutions and COO of Solcorp. Post Business School, he learned the business of selling as an executive at Xerox Corp. He lives in Toronto.